African Department

C000117244

FinTech in Sub-Saharan African Countries: A Game Changer?

Prepared by a staff team led by Amadou N. R. Sy
and composed of Rodolfo Maino, Alexander Massara,
Hector Perez-Saiz, and Preya Sharma

INTERNATIONAL MONETARY FUND

Cataloging-in-Publication Data

IMF Library

Names: Maino, Rodolfo, 1961-, author. | Massara, Alexander, author. | Perez-Saiz, Hector, author. | Sharma, Preya, author. | Sy, Amadou N. R., project director. | International Monetary Fund, publisher. | International Monetary Fund. African Department, issuing body.
Title: FinTech in sub-Saharan African countries: a game changer? / Prepared by an IMF Staff Team led by Amadou N. R. Sy and composed of Rodolfo Maino, Alexander Massara, Hector Perez-Saiz, and Preya Sharma.
Description: Washington, DC: International Monetary Fund, 2018. | At head of title: The African Department. | Includes bibliographical references.
Identifiers: ISBN 9781484385661 (paper)
Subjects: LCSH: Financial services industry—Technological innovations—Africa, Sub-Saharan. | Infrastructure (Economics)—Technological innovations—Africa, Sub-Saharan. | Africa, Sub-Saharan—Economic conditions.
Classification: LCC HC800.M35 2018

The Departmental Paper Series presents research by IMF staff on issues of broad regional or cross-country interest. The views expressed in this paper are those of the author(s) and do not necessarily represent the views of the IMF, its Executive Board, or IMF management.

Publication orders may be placed online, by fax, or through the mail:
International Monetary Fund, Publication Services
P.O. Box 92780, Washington, DC 20090, U.S.A.
Tel. (202) 623-7430 Fax: (202) 623-7201
E-mail: publications@imf.org
www.imfbookstore.org
www.elibrary.imf.org

Contents

Acknowledgments

This paper was written by a staff team led by Amadou Sy, including Rodolfo Maino, Alexander Massara, Hector Perez-Saiz, and Preya Sharma (all from the African Department). Cristina Piacentini was responsible for document production. The authors gratefully acknowledge the valuable comments received from Dong He, Dirk Jan Grolleman, David Jutrsa, and Tanai Khianonarong (all from the Monetary and Capital Markets Department, IMF), Roger Nord (Institute for Capacity Development, IMF), members of the IMF FinTech Group, and colleagues from the IMF.

Executive Summary

Financial technology (FinTech) is a major force shaping the structure of the financial industry in sub-Saharan Africa. New technologies are being developed and implemented in sub-Saharan Africa with the potential to change the competitive landscape in the financial sector. FinTech challenges traditional structures and creates efficiency gains by opening up the financial services value chain, although it also raises concerns about new vulnerabilities. Today, FinTech is emerging as a technological enabler in the region, improving financial inclusion and serving as a catalyst for innovation in other sectors, such as agriculture and infrastructure.

Sub-Saharan Africa has become the global leader in mobile money transfer services, spurring widespread access to financial services. Although sub-Saharan Africa has lagged behind the rest of the world in access to finance, some countries in the region are now global leaders. There is a wide degree of differences across the region, with East Africa leading in mobile money adoption and usage. Built on an appropriate pricing strategy to attract customers, suitable regulation, and a reliable and trustful network, Kenya represents today one of the most successful cases regarding the use of mobile money.

FinTech may carry significant gains for financial inclusion and deepening by improving the level of efficiency of the financial sector. FinTech provides avenues to extend access to credit as new technologies help overcome information barriers and lower the cost of cross-border transfers. In particular, pressures on correspondent banking relationships could be partly remedied by the use of new technologies if the new systems can satisfy requirements to avoid money laundering and the financing of terrorism. Furthermore, whereas the current technologies are still facing number of challenges, such as scalability and high energy consumption, future distributed ledger technologies could enhance efficiency, security, and transparency of payment systems in sub-Saharan Africa, thus lowering trading costs.

There is a need to balance the trade-off between the benefits that FinTech technologies may generate and potential added risks and vulnerabilities. Given the lower levels of financial inclusion, bank competition, and macro-financial linkages in sub-Saharan Africa relative to other regions, regulators and central banks could potentially benefit from considering FinTech as a leap-frogging opportunity to foster inclusive economic growth and development. At the same time, these new technologies and business models present new risks that would need to be addressed with suitable regulatory frameworks.

Policy measures are needed to reap the potential benefits of FinTech while managing associated risks. First, policymakers need to fill the large existing infrastructure gap in the region, starting with electricity and internet services. Second, there is a need to address the perennial race between fast-moving innovation and the slower pace of regulation. Third, policymakers should look beyond the potential benefits of FinTech in just the financial sector to consider the possible impact on employment and productivity, the digital economy, and more broadly, the scope for much needed structural transformation.

1 Introduction

Innovation in financial technology, often referred to as "FinTech," is rapidly transforming the global financial sector. Since 2010, more than US$50 billion has been invested in almost 2,500 companies worldwide as FinTech redefines the way in which we store, save, borrow, invest, move, spend, and protect money (Skan, Dickerson, and Gagliardi 2016). Although there is not yet a consensus, the working definition of FinTech adopted by the Financial Stability Board points to "technologically enabled financial innovation that could result in new business models, applications, processes, or products with an associated material effect on financial markets and institutions and the provision of financial services" (Financial Stability Board 2017).

Ongoing innovation in business models and processes is building on advances in technology. The technological basis for new FinTech business models and services rests on the development of some major innovations developed in recent decades. These include distributed computing, artificial intelligence, big data, cryptography, smart contracts, and mobile internet access. Taken together, these innovations have enabled the ability to collate and analyze vast amounts of data, develop more robust security systems, and connect economic agents through multiple types of platforms on a real-time basis.

FinTech is challenging traditional structures and is creating efficiency gains by opening up the financial services value chain. Much of the interest in FinTech is related to the way in which innovation in the financial sector can lead to increased access, better services, and gains in efficiency. Such innovation includes transforming all aspects of delivery of core functions of the financial sector such as settling payments, facilitating borrowing and saving, risk sharing, and allocating capital. Moreover, this process could trigger deep changes to the existing market structure and financial market infrastructure for the provision of these services. The current financial infrastructure typically revolves around (1) incumbent banks, serving retail, commercial, and wholesale customers; (2) insurance and pension providers; and (3) money, foreign exchange, and capital markets, all of which are underpinned by payment system providers and other financial market providers, as well as central banks and regulators. Financial innovation can improve the way the private and public sectors function.

FinTech has the potential to strengthen and accelerate important gains in financial development achieved in sub-Saharan Africa over the past two decades. Financial liberalization, reform of monetary policy frameworks and instruments, and improvements in the institutional environment contributed to a significant expansion of banking activities and financial products. Some countries achieved decisive progress in financial deepening and now have increased access to international financial markets, while others have lagged. The advent of pan-African banks led to an increased use of payment system tools such as debit and credit cards, and there has been robust growth in mobile payments in many countries. Still, financial systems in sub-Saharan Africa face several limitations and financial inclusion remains too narrow, limiting the prospect for further gains in sustained growth, employment, and poverty reduction.

While acknowledging the large potential gains from FinTech, there are concerns about new vulnerabilities that these technologies and business models may bring. New competitors without previous experience in the industry are providing innovative financial services. For instance, blockchain-based technology promises to enhance trust in economic exchanges. Its applications are designed to provide a secure digital infrastructure to verify identity, facilitate faster and cheaper cross-border payments, and protect property rights.[1] However, these technologies may be rapidly creating new types of risks that are not well understood or covered by existing regulations.

Against this background, a careful consideration of the potential of FinTech is needed to boost banking and financial development in sub-Saharan Africa.[2] It is necessary to balance the trade-off between the potential benefits that FinTech generates and the added vulnerabilities that may be created. However, given the low level of financial inclusion and competition in Africa, and more limited macro-financial linkages relative to other world regions, regulators and central banks should seriously consider FinTech as an opportunity to fos-

---

[1]Pisa and Juden (2017) discuss in detail the potential role of blockchain technology in addressing development challenges.

[2]In October 2018, the International Monetary Fund and the World Bank Group (2018) launched the Bali FinTech Agenda, a set of 12 policy elements aimed at helping member countries harness the benefits and opportunities of rapid advances in financial technology that are transforming the provision of banking services, while at the same time managing the inherent risks. The Agenda proposes a framework of high-level issues that countries should consider in their own domestic policy discussions and aims to guide staff from the two institutions in their own work and dialogue with national authorities.

ter economic growth and development. The rest of the paper is organized as follows: Chapter 2 discusses the trends and unique characteristics of FinTech in sub-Saharan Africa. Chapter 3 explains the opportunities and challenges that FinTech creates in sub-Saharan Africa. Chapter 4 concludes.

2 FinTech in Sub-Saharan Africa—Where Does the Region Stand?

Financial intermediation and financial inclusion in sub-Saharan Africa remain low, despite progress in recent years. Helped by reforms, the depth and coverage of financial systems in sub-Saharan Africa—as measured by the standard indicators of financial development, such as the ratios of private sector credit to GDP and broad money to GDP—have significantly improved over the period 1995 to 2013 (Kasekende 2010). However, on average, countries in sub-Saharan Africa continue to have a shallower financial system than those in other developing regions of the world (Figure 1). In terms of financial inclusion, only 20 percent of the population has a bank account compared to 92 percent in advanced economies and 38 percent in nonadvanced economies (Table 1). Underinvestment, poor infrastructure, and comparatively low levels of financial literacy have contributed to the region being underbanked.

However, mobile money has underpinned a radical change in the delivery of financial services in sub-Saharan Africa. As a result, the region has become the global leader in mobile money innovation, adoption, and usage, with close to 40 out of 45 sub-Saharan African countries actively using this new financial technology (FinTech).[1] Within sub-Saharan Africa, East Africa continues to lead in terms of adoption and usage rates. Whereas overall financial depth remains below other regions, FinTech is emerging as an engine of growth and technological enabler that fosters financial inclusion and economic development.

---

[1]Both the Middle East, North Africa, Afghanistan, and Pakistan, and Caucasus and Central Asia regions are also reporting progress in the adoption of FinTech. See Lukonga (2018).

Figure 1. Indicators of Financial Development

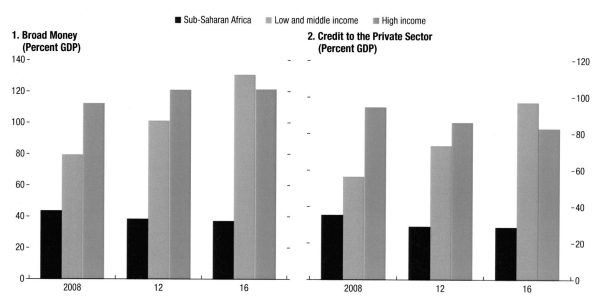

Source: World Bank, World Development Indicators database.

Sub-Saharan Africa Leads the World in Mobile Money

The widespread use of mobile money has transformed the delivery of financial services in sub-Saharan Africa.[2] Sub-Saharan Africa leads the world in mobile money accounts per capita (both registered and active accounts), mobile money outlets, and volume of mobile money transactions (Figure 2). Mobile money account penetration in sub-Saharan African countries recorded a remarkable increase of almost 20 percent between 2011 and 2014,

Table 1. Key Financial and Development Indicators
(2017 or latest available)

	Sub-Saharan Africa	Low & Middle Income	High Income
Bank or mobile money account (% of population ages 15+)	43	63	94
ATMs (per 100,000 adults)	6	27	68
Commercial bank branches (per 100,000 adults)	5	9	20
Fixed broadband subscriptions (per 100 people)	1	9	31
GDP per capita, PPP (current international $)	3,730	10,345	45,789
Mobile cellular subscriptions (per 100 people)	73	96	126

Source: World Bank, World Development Indicators database.

---

[2]Mobile money is understood as a digital medium of exchange and store of value facilitated by mobile agents, is stored in mobile money accounts, and is accessible through mobile phones. Mobile money facilitates low-cost and small-scale transactions, expanding access to financial services beyond those offered by alternative financial service providers, including digital banking.

Figure 2. Mobile Money Indicators
(Regional averages, 2017 or latest available)

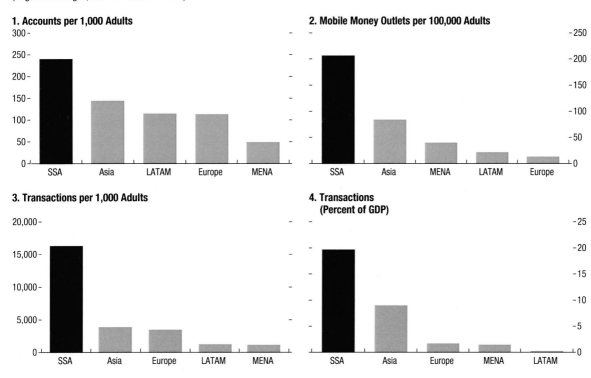

Source: IMF Financial Access Survey.
Note: LATAM = Latin America; MENA = Middle East and North Africa; SSA = sub-Saharan Africa.

largely driven by ongoing financial innovation. In addition, close to 10 percent of GDP in transactions are occurring through mobile money, compared with just 7 percent of GDP in Asia and less than 2 percent of GDP in other regions. Most transactions are used to send and receive domestic remittances. Increasingly, transactions are also being used for domestic transfers such as paying utility bills, receiving wages, and payments for goods and services (Figure 3).

Mobile money accounts have now overtaken traditional bank accounts in several sub-Saharan African economies. Based on data for 17 sub-Saharan African countries for which both mobile money and traditional bank account data is available, there were nearly twice as many traditional deposit accounts as mobile money accounts in 2012. By 2015, mobile money accounts surpassed traditional deposit accounts in these 17 economies, which include some of the largest in sub-Saharan Africa, such as South Africa, Kenya, and Tanzania (Figure 4).

Figure 3. Uses of Mobile Money in Sub-Saharan Africa

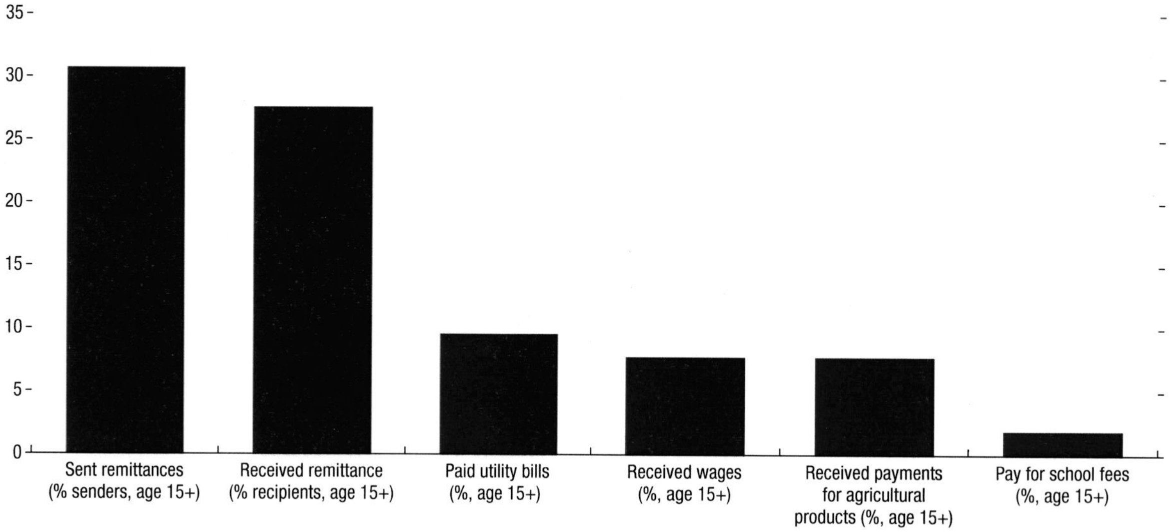

Source: Global Findex.

Figure 4. Mobile Money Developments in Sub-Saharan Africa

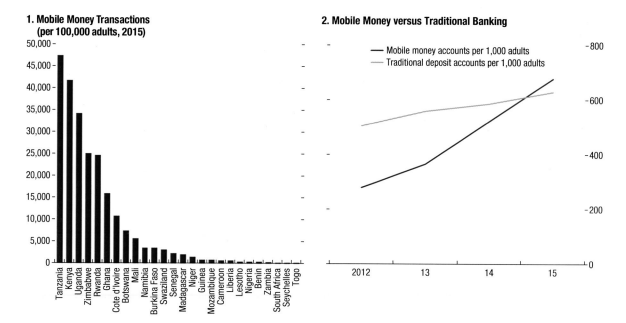

Source: IMF Financial Access Survey.

Factors for Success

The success of mobile payments in sub-Saharan Africa is the result of several factors (Box 1). The low number of branches and automatic teller machines (ATMs) in the region and the absence of internet connections makes it difficult to transfer remittances or pay bills. Therefore, there is a large unfulfilled demand for payments services, and the relatively large penetration of mobile devices in the region provides a technological platform that can be used by mobile money agents.[3] In fact, there are now more mobile money agents in sub-Saharan Africa than ATMs or bank accounts.[4]

Within sub-Saharan Africa, East Africa is the clear leader in mobile money adoption and usage. Despite the success of mobile money in sub-Saharan Africa, there is a wide degree of cross-country difference (see Figure 4). East Africa developed an infrastructure that uniquely built upon the latent demand for mobile financial services in sub-Saharan Africa:

- East African countries favored a telecom-led regulatory model. In this framework, the telecom provider works with the financial regulator to establish the infrastructure for mobile payments. The telecom-led model has proved more successful in attracting users than the bank-led model that other sub-Saharan Africa countries promoted.
- East African countries tended to have a single telecom provider with a large market share, which provided an initial critical mass of users needed to push mobile money past the niche level. In Kenya, Safaricom has a share of nearly 70 percent of the market; in Tanzania, Vodacom has a market share of close to half. Having a large market share allowed most mobile payment users to operate on a single platform without facing compatibility issues, though this raises concentration and potential stability concerns.
- East African countries, particularly in the East African Community, have national identification systems. These systems facilitate faster mobile payment adoption rates and enable more secure transactions.

Addressing the region's infrastructure gap can lead to an even higher usage of mobile payment and other financial services. Sub-Saharan Africa lags behind the rest of the world not only in terms of access to electricity but also in terms of internet penetration and technological readiness (Table 2). For a sample of sub-Saharan African countries, as of 2017, 388 million of the continent's 1.25 billion are online, with 160 million holding Facebook accounts. All sub-Saharan African countries score relatively low on the technological

---

[3]The GSM Association defines a mobile agent as a person or business contracted to process mobile transactions for users. Agents usually earn commissions for performing this service and often provide frontline customer service, such as teaching new users how to complete transactions on their phone.

[4]Dupas et al. (2016) show that distance to banks acts as a barrier to access financial services.

Table 2. Sub-Saharan Africa: Internet Penetration and Technological Readiness, 2017

Country	Population (millions)	Internet Penetration (percent of population)	Technological Readiness 2017 (scale 0–7)	Facebook Users, June 2012 (millions)	Increase in Facebook Users, 2012–17 (percent)
Algeria	41.1	45.2	3.4	18.0	339
Angola	26.5	22.3	NA	3.8	533
Cameroon	24.5	25.0	2.6	2.1	250
Côte d'Ivoire	23.8	26.5	NA	2.4	NA
Ethiopia	104.3	15.4	2.4	4.5	400
Ghana	28.6	34.7	3.6	4.0	150
Kenya	48.5	46.0	3.7	6.2	210
Morocco	35.2	58.3	3.8	12.0	135
Mozambique	29.5	17.5	2.9	1.4	250
Nigeria	191.8	47.7	3.0	16.0	142
Senegal	16.0	25.7	3.3	2.3	228
South Africa	55.4	54.0	4.6	16.0	153
Tanzania	56.8	10.7	2.6	6.1	771

Source: Internet Society (2017).
Note: NA = not available.

readiness pillar of the World Bank's *Global Competitiveness Report 2017*. Therefore, the margin of improvement for the continent is large, and the potential impact of new technologies and infrastructure can set the path for much stronger and inclusive financial development in the region. In many instances, telecoms benefit from high barriers to entry, resulting in highly concentrated segments. Although size matters for some telecoms to manage liquidity and counterparty risk, from a policy perspective it is critical to lower costs, improve access, and facilitate interoperability to foster competition. In this regard, the proliferation of taxes on the telecoms sector in recent years— like customs duties on capital equipment and handsets, diverse regulatory fees, high corporate income tax and value-added tax rates, or telephone call excises—may distort product and output markets, impeding efficiency, affordability, and growth.[5]

FinTech Promotes Financial Inclusion Beyond the Payments Arena

A well-functioning payment system is indispensable to reduce the costs of exchanging goods and services in the economy. However, promoting financial inclusion and development implies going beyond payments. There is broad demand in the region for many other financial services that are underdeveloped, such as the provision of several types of credit services, cross-border payments, various forms of investment products, and insurance services.

FinTech providers are leveraging their experience and large customer base in payments services to provide other financial services. Helped by a large customer base and a mature technological platform, some mobile pay-

[5]For an analysis of the economic rationale for sector-specific taxes on telecommunications, see Matheson and Petit (2017).

Figure 5. Alternative Finance Volume by Model in Africa, 2013–15

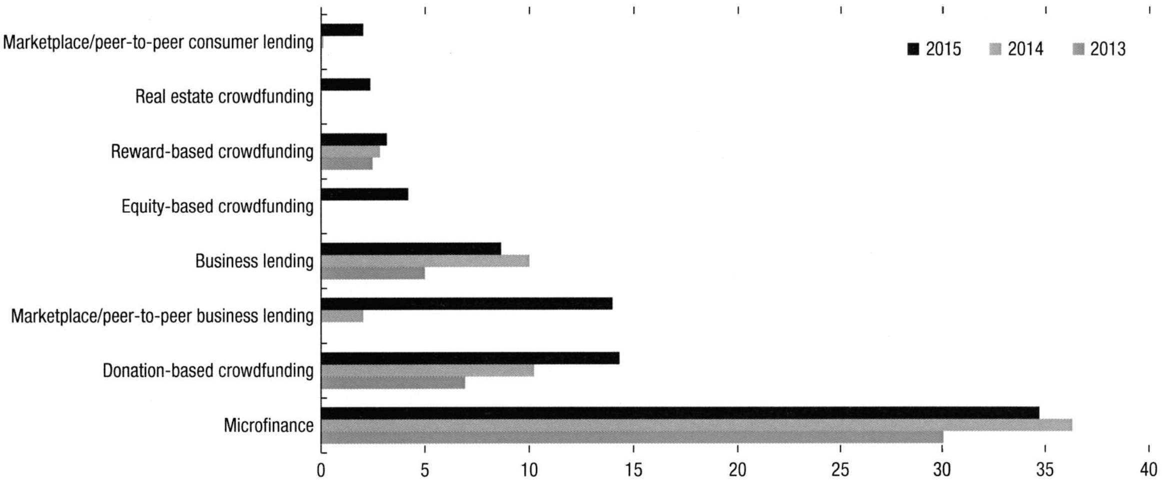

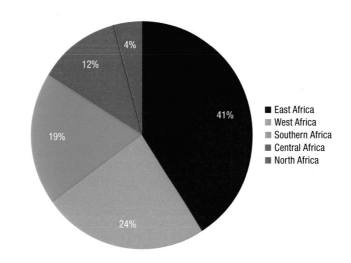

Source: Cambridge Centre for Alternative Finance (2017).

ment providers can efficiently provide new financial services. Indeed, more advanced types of FinTech, centered on lending rather than payments, are growing throughout sub-Saharan Africa. While microfinance has traditionally led the region as an alternate source of finance, in recent years FinTech has facilitated the growth of several types of crowdfunding and peer-to-peer lending (Figure 5). As with mobile payments, East Africa leads the region in the use of these alternate financing sources (Figure 6). Box 2 provides several

Figure 6. Regional Distribution of Alternative Finance in Sub-Saharan Africa

Source: Andresen (2017).

11

examples of financial services platforms in sub-Saharan Africa that go beyond mobile money.

From Financial Deepening to Economic Development

FinTech is emerging as a technological enabler in the region. FinTech is not only helping improve financial inclusion in the region, but it also serves as a catalyst for the emergence of innovations in other sectors, such as agriculture and infrastructure, which promotes economic growth and development. FinTech may also complement other nonfinancial technologies and foster innovation by the government, setting the path for the development of a digital economy in the region (see Box 3).

Box 1. Why Kenya?

M-Pesa (M for mobile, pesa means *money* in Kiswahili) is a mobile phone–based money transfer system that was launched in 2007 by Safaricom and Vodacom, the largest mobile network operators in Kenya and Tanzania, who are owned by Vodafone. M-Pesa was jointly developed by the UK Department for International Development and Voda-fone in the early 2000s. The service has been successful as it allows customers to deposit and withdraw money, transfer money to other users, or pay bills. The service quickly expanded to other countries in sub-Saharan Africa including Tanzania, Lesotho, Mozam-bique, and Ghana, and also Albania, Roma-nia, and India. As of end-2016, the service had almost 30 million users worldwide, of which 20.7 million are in Kenya. Today, Kenya is one of the economies with the highest use of mobile money at 53 transac-tions per adult per year (Figure 7).

There are several reasons for the high success of this service (see Mas and Ng'weno [2010] and Mas and Radcliffe [2011]):

Figure 7. Mobile Money Developments in Kenya

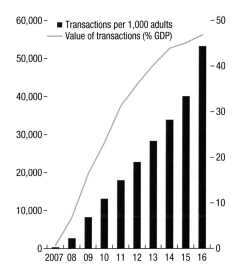

Source: Financial Access Survey.

1. The low level of financial market infra-structure (branches, automatic teller machines, payment systems) generates a large unfulfilled demand for payment services in a market segment with a rela-tively large level of access to mobile devices. In addition, a good market strategy is necessary to successfully deploy a service that is often subject to significant barriers related to network effects, the "chicken-and-egg" trap, and lack of trust (Evans and Schmalensee 2016; Shapiro and Varian 1998).

2. An appropriate pricing strategy to attract customers and stores in tandem, and the deployment of a reliable and trustful network, are critical for success.

3. Safaricom had a good working relationship with the Central Bank of Kenya and was given regulatory space to design M-Pesa in a manner that fit its mar-ket; this provided sufficient prudential comfort to the central bank. A recent study by Suri and Jack (2016) underlined the role of M-Pesa to achieve inclusive growth in Kenya.

Box 1. Why Kenya *(continued)*

Going forward, mobile money can accelerate the inclusion of users into the formal financial system by integrating mobile money and other financial services providers. In Kenya, mobile network operators partner with banks, creating a hybrid system that offers access to formal saving, loan, and insurance products such as Safaricom's M-Shwari, which provides access to savings accounts and instantaneous micro-credit products.

Box 2. From Payments to Credit and Saving Products in Sub-Saharan Africa

Financial technology (FinTech) providers often start with simple high-demand services and then leverage economies of density and a strong reputation in the country to expand their portfolio of products by providing related banking services, such as credit or saving products. The industry is growing rapidly and the examples that follow—although not exhaustive—illustrate the fast pace of innovation in the region.

Founded in 2009, **Paga** offers digital bank services (peer-to-peer money transfer, bill payments, online payments, and payroll), achieving a wide reach in Nigeria.

SimbaPay is a UK-based digital money transfer service serving Kenya, Uganda, Nigeria, and Ghana that delivers money via existing mobile money wallet services and using its SimbaPay app. Simbapay and Kenya's Family Bank recently launched an instant payment service from East Africa to China. Users can send funds to China through Family Bank's **PesaPap** app or Safaricom's **M-Pesa**.

Orange Money offers a payment and withdrawal card (Visa card) in Botswana, Cameroon, and Côte d'Ivoire, and **Orange Bank Africa** has been created in partnership with bancassurance group NSIA. **Orange Group** and **MTN Group**, two of Africa's largest mobile operators and mobile money providers, set up a joint venture, **Mowali** (mobile wallet interoperability), that enables interoperable payments across Africa.

Zoona is a mobile payments company that has expanded its portfolio of banking products beyond payments. Zoona offers the service **Sunga Pockets** that helps customers to store money in an affordable and accessible electronic account.

Zoona has also partnered with **Kiva**, a crowdlending platform, to offer entrepreneurs financial support. The Kiva platform gives individuals from around the world the opportunity to offer small loans to entrepreneurs. The entrepreneurs are vetted by Kiva and over time the loans are repaid. Lenders are given the choice to keep their loan within the system to support more entrepreneurs or withdraw it once they are satisfied with the entrepreneur's progress.

Wizzit is a payments company that has started providing microfinance products (see International Finance Corporation 2011). Building on its payment services (mobile payments to more than 7 million people in 13 countries for more than 15 years), Wizzit partnered with the World Bank Group to create a microfinance pilot to allow users to access microloans through their phones for personal use or to grow their small

---

The information on financial technology providers is for illustrative purposes only and is not intended to serve as an investment advice or a formal endorsement.

Box 2. From Payments to Credit and Saving Products in Sub-Saharan Africa *(continued)*

businesses. Since 2015, **Wizall**, a Senegalese start-up, provides electronic payments and money transfer services in West Africa.

GetBucks provides microfinance products such as personal loans for terms of up to six months. It uses a platform called FinCloud to provide financial services through the internet, mobile phones, and other channels.

Box 3. Digital Innovation and Financial Services in Sub-Saharan Africa

The words "Africa" and "innovation" are not often found in the same sentence. But in fact, much is happening in Africa. The reach of mobile networks and growth in subscriptions have made mobile technology the go-to means by which digital content and services are created and consumed. Several sub-Saharan African countries have established hubs for tech start-ups and have generated new employment opportunities. These hubs provide the means for the industry to continue evolving not only in size but in variety of services offered.

Innovation in the agricultural sector has huge potential in Africa. Digital financial services increase smallholder farmers' access to weather and market information and help decision making on when and which crops to plant and where to sell crops. The Tigo Kilimo SMS-based application, launched in Tanzania in 2012, provides up-to-date weather and agronomic information, and the Connected Farmer program in East Africa sends up-to-date market prices to farmers' mobile phones, allowing them to select the best markets and times at which to sell, and receive digital payments and receipts.

In fragile and conflict-affected states, financial technology (FinTech) has played an instrumental role. In Sierra Leone, the government turned to mobile wallets to help fight the Ebola virus outbreak. The United Nations finds that mobile payments to emergency workers dramatically shortened payment times and minimized fraud during the outbreak. In Liberia, mobile payments to health and education workers who work in areas periodically cut off during the rainy season have helped maintain critical social services. FinTech is also increasingly being harnessed to improve tax collection, thereby contributing to domestic revenue mobilization, a key objective in many African countries.

Payments innovation has also benefited the health sector. In Rwanda, the government has partnered with a private company (Zipline) to use drones guided by mobile phone–based location services to quickly deliver life-saving medical products to rural health clinics. Payment by mobile phone facilitates the business model.

New technology also has the potential to help address Africa's infrastructure deficit. M-Kopa Solar in Kenya (Kopa means borrow in Kiswahili) sells solar home systems on a payment plan, with an initial deposit followed by daily payments up to one year. After completing payments, customers own the product outright. M-Kopa aims at solving two problems simultaneously: it seeks to accelerate rural electrification, a big challenge in sparsely populated African countries, and to provide consumer credit to rural households who would have found it difficult to qualify for a loan from a traditional bank.

Box 3. Digital Innovation and Financial Services in Sub-Saharan Africa *(continued)*

Blockchain technologies can potentially be applied to many other environments beyond virtual currencies. Bitland is a new platform in Ghana that seeks to solve the endemic problem of land registration (as much as 90 percent of agricultural land is reportedly undocumented). Bitland creates a record for every piece of land that is stored on a blockchain, and thereby renders them less susceptible to forgery or tampering. In principle, out-of-court settlements of land disputes should be quicker and easier with the use of blockchain technology.

3 FinTech-led Transformations and Implications

As the financial technology (FinTech) space is developing, innovators are seeking to enhance elements along the financial services value chain well beyond mobile money. Start-ups, established players, and central banks are in a process of discovery to design, test, and re-design new products, services, and regulation. Underpinning this process is the coalescence of new technologies. The largest impact will occur in the financial sector with important implications for broader growth. This chapter seeks to provide a guide to considering the channels through which the future financial development of FinTech in sub-Saharan Africa could occur and the policy implications in terms of the trade-offs FinTech could create.

FinTech represents a disruptive competitive force that will have a major role in shaping the structure of the financial industry. FinTech primarily affects market structure by bringing new technologies that (1) reduce the costs of financial services, (2) create market access opportunities for new entrants (nonbanks), (3) broaden access to new segments of the market and customers, and (4) affect the competitiveness of existing incumbents. These changes may potentially create large efficiency gains in an industry that has not experienced major technological and market structure changes in the last decades.

The technological foundations for these new products and services are well developed. The products and services being created in the field of FinTech draw on global technological innovations. Broadly, these include the following (see He et al. 2017):

- Mobile access and the internet connect consumers to firms and to each other (person-to-person transactions).
- Big data and artificial intelligence comprise the availability and analysis of databases that have billions of observations of transactions and char-

acteristics, which can be used to help design and tailor financial products and services.

- Distributed ledger technology (DLT) refers to a type of networking of independent computers to record, share, and synchronize transactions rather than have a centralized database.[1]
- Cryptography allows for robust security systems that enable electronic transactions to be carried out safely and is the basis for smart contracts and cryptocurrencies.

The application of these new technologies in sub-Saharan Africa offers transformational potential. Although it is difficult to provide a comprehensive set of changes that could occur, these new technologies can help to reduce existing market inefficiencies. Together these technological developments provide avenues to reduce information costs, increase transparency, as well as enable greater trust and enforcement of contracts (Box 4).[2] The new technologies will also bring a range of risks that will need to be mitigated.

Possible Transformations: Financial Inclusion and Deepening

FinTech can have a significant impact on financial inclusion and deepening by improving the level of efficiency of the industry. Sub-Saharan Africa has lower levels of financial inclusion and depth compared to other emerging market and developing economies. This provides space for significant growth opportunities in the sector as there is a large proportion of the population that does not have access to financial services. FinTech offers opportunities to new entrepreneurs and incumbents in the financial sector that can leverage innovative and less costly business models to serve this large uncovered segment of the market. In particular, the relatively large penetration of mobile phones (81 mobile phones per 100 inhabitants) gives new entrants a unique opportunity to reach these new customers with mobile-based financial services.

Access to credit could also be extended through technologies that overcome information barriers. The cost of credit risk assessment remains high in sub-Saharan Africa. Challenges for banks stem from unreliable accounting and financial information, a lack of credit bureaus, and limitations in legal institutions. Small- and medium-sized enterprises (SMEs) cite access to finance as their main challenge, which has also gender equality implications

---

[1]A distributed ledger is a distributed database where each node has a synchronized copy of the data, allowing also for (1) decentralization (control of the database is done by all network participants), (2) reliable trust-less environments, and (3) cryptographic encryption. See more at Benos, Garratt, and Gurrola-Perez (2017).

[2]See also Figure 4 from the He et al. (2017), which provides a mapping of the major technologies and how they impact financial services.

Table 3. Competition Indicators by Region

Indicator	Sub-Saharan Africa	Other non advanced economies	Advanced economies
Boone	−0.04	−0.06	−0.08
C5	82.5	77.4	84.2
H statistic	0.49	0.55	0.60
Lerner	0.31	0.30	0.25

Source: World Bank, World Development Indicators database (2011).
Notes: The maximum value of the Boone indicator is 0 (monopoly case) and the more negative it is, the higher the level of competition. The C5 is the combined market share of the five largest financial institutions in a country. The H-statistic is zero under monopoly, and the greater it is, the higher the degree of competition. The Lerner index is zero under perfect competition and the higher it is, the less competition in the market.

as women-owned SMEs are even more limited in getting access to credit. Big data and machine learning, for instance, has the potential to reduce the cost of credit risk assessments, particularly in countries that do not have an established credit registry. This can be achieved by using a broader range of information such as mobile phone usage data and payments data, which is available in higher volume, and new statistical tools to process this larger volume of information to better understand and measure the nature of credit risks. Such alternative information for credit risk assessments, possibly at a lower cost, in sub-Saharan Africa could attract new entrants into the provision of credit, including (non-deposit-taking) FinTech firms (peer-to-peer and other crowdfunding platforms). This will have implications for competition and the use of personal information by third-party players and carry legal and regulatory risks.

FinTech can change the financial industry in sub-Saharan Africa by increasing competition and efficiency. Bank competition in Africa is low compared to other regions of the world (Table 3 and Figure 8). Bazot (2018) and Philippon (2016) argue that the current financial system has historically been inefficient. Moreover, banks in sub-Saharan Africa are typically less efficient than banks in other world regions and, therefore, financial services are more expensive. This inefficiency is driven in part by higher operational costs (Beck and Cull 2014). Lower competition in these countries may be the result of high entry barriers due to the existence of a negative business climate or the regulatory barriers. New FinTech entrants may face lower entry barriers as they may require a smaller scale of operation to be profitable.

Broader financial development in sub-Saharan Africa could be pushed forward at an accelerated pace. There is a need to develop financial markets in sub-Saharan Africa beyond retail payments; the banking sector and financial market infrastructure as capital markets, insurance companies, pension funds, and other financial institutions and instruments remain limited. The level of financial literacy remains relatively low in sub-Saharan Africa. Efforts are underway in the region to use FinTech for users to pay insurance premiums (Lesotho), receive pension payments (Ghana), and purchase government

21

Figure 8. Competition (Lerner Index) by Region

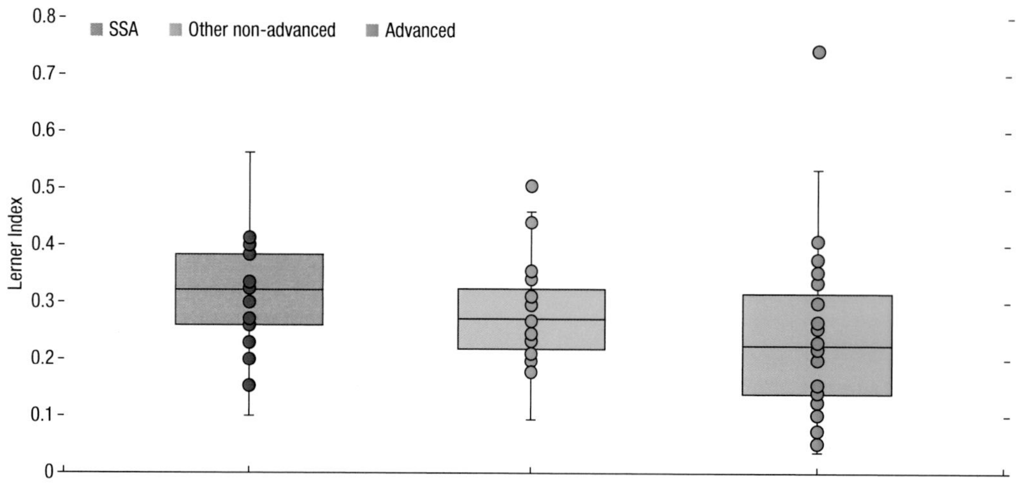

Source: Authors' calculations.

securities (Kenya). FinTech tools can also help support financial literacy programs (electronic wallet, education at the primary school and higher levels).

Possible Transformations: Cross-Border and Domestic Payments

A potential widespread application of FinTech could be to significantly lower the cost of cross-border transfers. The cost of sending remittances to sub-Saharan Africa is the highest globally (see Ratha et al. 2018) in part because of the oligopolistic nature of the banking industry in sub-Saharan Africa, low regional and financial integration, and the existence of multiple currencies and inefficient payment systems for intra-African cross-border payments. FinTech has the potential to reduce transaction costs with positive effects on the volume of remittances and regional integration. DLTs are being considered to facilitate value transfer exchanges between parties without the need for cross-border intermediation. Network technologies could have the potential to bypass the complex web of intermediaries present in these cross-border payments (multiple correspondent banks or infrastructures such as continuous linked settlement [CLS]).[3,4] Intermediaries can also use such technologies.[5]

---

[3]For instance, international payments using cryptocurrencies can be securely received in minutes and can be rapidly settled in the domestic currency. DLT systems such as Ripple can be used to efficiently process foreign payments and can be supported by international banks and payment companies.

[4]CLS is a global clearing and settlement system for cross-border foreign exchange transactions. The system is operated by CLS Bank International, which is owned by over 70 global banking and financial institutions. It enables foreign exchange transactions involving the CLS eligible currencies to be settled through the CLS System on a payment-versus-payment basis, thus eliminating the settlement risk in these transactions.

[5]For instance, CLS has started using a DLT platform.

Pressures on correspondent banking relationships could also be partly remedied by new technologies. Cross-border flows, including those related to trade and remittances, are being challenged in many countries by the loss of correspondent banking relations. The current correspondent banking relations model is also expensive as correspondent banks often need to maintain liquidity (prefunding) at correspondent banks and enter in credit relationships with them (overdrafts). In addition, there has been an increase in compliance costs, including in relation to sanctions regimes and anti-money laundering and combating the financing of terrorism (AML/CFT). Such a model can also entail long payment chains, particularly in the context of nested relationships. These ongoing pressures on correspondent banking relationships have mostly affected transactions denominated in US dollars. In some instances, FinTech solutions could offer cost savings and secure solutions (for example, certain regulation-focused technologies) that facilitate customer due diligence measures and information sharing for the purpose of correspondent banking relationships. Other emerging FinTech solutions (for example, blockchain technology) could provide a more efficient alternative to the traditional correspondent banking model. Provided the new systems can still satisfy the international AML/CFT standards, this could be a substantial boost to low-income countries that receive significant remittances from overseas.

DLT could enhance efficiency of certain types of payment systems in sub-Saharan Africa. With DLT, all operations are jointly kept by all members of the network and all processes involving ordering, settlement, and payments are implemented in real time. Currently in payment systems across sub-Saharan Africa, settlement processes that are not operated in real-time (non–real-time gross settlement systems), may involve several days to be fully executed, thus increasing operational costs and creating operational and counterparty risk. DLT could speed up the settlement of transactions with a decentralized and automated settlement process, thus reducing back-office costs. However, it should be noted that use of DLT for wholesale payments brings its own specific set of operational risks and some limitation on scalability. Some central banks in sub-Saharan Africa are actively experimenting with DLT-based payment systems. For example, the South African Reserve Bank initiated a proof of concept that simulated a "real-world" trial of a DLT-based wholesale payment system using a tokenized South African rand (Box 5).

Possible Transformations: Fiscal and Monetary Sectors

Some of the innovations in finance could be applied to the fiscal sector to improve the efficiency of the interaction between the state and citizens. A

23

longstanding challenge in many sub-Saharan African countries is the efficient collection of taxes and delivery of public services and social spending. For example, estimates suggest that digitalizing government payments could create value of roughly 1 percent of GDP for most countries (Gupta et al. 2017). If well implemented, there are potential gains in tax administration and compliance, targeting of social programs, and public financial management, more broadly using existing data on transactions and combining it with personal information. Public procurement could also benefit from the use of smart contracts that are designed to facilitate, verify, or enforce contract negotiations or performance. As with existing fiscal operations, effective systems would need measures to protect privacy and minimize generating new methods for fraud and evasion. Moreover, the use of DLT could offer tools to help promote transparency and reduce corruption.

If adopted widely, digital currencies could have profound implications for the monetary sector. It has been argued that some digital currencies and other forms of digital money could potentially replace traditional currencies. The economic literature has widely cited the three economic functions of money: (1) medium of exchange, (2) unit of account, and (3) store of value. Digital currencies issued by the private sector differ along many dimensions and, at the moment, struggle to fully satisfy the functions of money, in part because of erratic valuations. In addition, they pose considerable risks as potential vehicles for money laundering, terrorism financing, tax evasion, fraud, and other financial crimes. Unlike private sector issuance of a digital currency, state issuance would satisfy the three functions of money and could further support public policy goals such as financial inclusion, security and consumer protection, and ensuring a degree of privacy in payments (Mancini-Griffoli et al. 2018). Even then, there are potential downsides of a digital currency, including risks to financial integrity and stability, that should be considered, as well as concerns from central banks regarding the implications of the broader adoption of digital currencies[6] and how this could affect the implementation of monetary policy (Heller 2017a, 2017b; Box 6).[7]

---

[6]The Committee on Payments and Market Infrastructures and the Markets Committee recently completed work on central bank digital currencies, analyzing their potential implications for payment systems, monetary policy implementation and transmission, as well as for the structure and stability of the financial system. The report underlines that wholesale central bank digital currencies, combined with the use of DLT, may enhance settlement efficiency for transactions involving securities and derivatives, but central banks should carefully monitor digital innovations (Committee on Payments and Market Infrastructures 2014, 2016; Committee on Payments and Market Infrastructures and Markets Committee 2018).

[7]The use of e-money could also affect the production, design, and distribution of currency, which is today a traditional area of responsibility for central banks.

The Need for Investing in Hard and Soft Infrastructure

FinTech and associated innovations can have macroeconomic gains for sub-Saharan African countries and make growth more inclusive. Increased and more efficient financial intermediation can have a positive impact on growth (see the finance and growth literature pioneered by Levine [2005]), especially if access to credit by SMEs increases. In addition, in economies dominated by the informal sector, new technologies can increase the incentives to formalize (for instance, electronic payment of taxes in exchange for being included in a pension system).

Investment in hard and soft infrastructure is needed to enable FinTech to develop and serve a rapidly growing digital generation. Hard infrastructure refers to the need for investment in internet connections and energy to enable firms to gain from the technological improvements. Soft infrastructure relates to the need for regulation to support a favorable business environment and investment in skills.

Allocating resources to these investments will require policymakers in sub-Saharan Africa to address several trade-offs. Estimates for investment in hard infrastructure are already large and pressing, whereas rising levels of public indebtedness limits the scope of public financing. Filling the large existing hard infrastructure gap in the region will require considering how to work with the private sector to provide financing or delivery of services for the adequate provision of electricity and internet services.

Investment in soft infrastructure needs to address the perennial race between fast-moving innovation and the slower pace of regulation. There is a trade-off between catalyzing, or at least supporting, rapid innovation, which has large potential gains to the economy, and taking the time to identify and manage its associated risks through regulation and supervision to ensure financial stability and integrity (Box 7). Given the central importance of financial regulation in supporting the growth of the FinTech sector, the following chapter gives deeper consideration to these factors.

Soft Infrastructure: Rethinking Financial Sector Regulation

A variety of FinTech developments, especially related to the regulatory and supervisory sector ("RegTech" and "SupTech," respectively), can potentially strengthen financial stability by increasing diversification and transparency as well as enabling better assessment of risks by all players in the financial sector (Box 8).

Table 4. Financial Technology: Benefits and Risks

Benefits	Encourages decentralization and diversification, dampening the effects of financial shocks in the event of a failure of an institution. Increases transparency and enables risks to be more accurately assessed and better price. Improves financial inclusion of households and small businesses.
Risks	Vulnerability of financial technology firms to micro-financial risks, stemming from both financial (such as maturity mismatch, liquidity mismatch, and leverage) and operational (such as governance, cyber, and common third-party reliance) sources. Propagation to the rest of the financial sector through unforeseen channels. Exacerbation of system-wide macro-financial risks, such as contagion, procyclicality, or excess volatility, which can amplify shocks to the financial system.

Source: Financial Stability Board (2017).

At the same time, potential gains from the emergence of FinTech carry risks and introduce new vulnerabilities. Safety and soundness considerations are a concern as the financial sector is prone to crises, panics, or runs (Table 4 and Box 9). Market failures such as externalities and asymmetric information exacerbate the effects of these financial shocks, which may propagate to the rest of the financial system and the entire economy, as well as create perverse feedback loops with the financial system. FinTech can exacerbate some of the well-known existing vulnerabilities or create new weaknesses that were not previously present in the financial system (see Basel Committee on Banking Supervision 2017). Among the 10 areas of risk identified by the Financial Stability Board, 3 are priorities for international collaboration with relevance in sub-Saharan Africa: (1) the need to manage operational risk from third-party service providers, (2) mitigating cyber-risks, and (3) monitoring macro-financial risks that could emerge as FinTech activities increase.[8]

Some steps are being taken in sub-Saharan Africa to start addressing these risks. For instance, the Central Bank of Kenya (CBK) issued information and telecommunications technology risk management guidelines to the banking sector in 2012 followed by a cybersecurity guidance note to the banking sector in 2017. The CBK has subsequently extended the coverage of cybersecurity guidelines to payment service providers through its 2018 draft guidelines. In addition to guidance on cyber-risks issues, the CBK has emphasized supervision, collaboration with national agencies, and information security in its strategy to mitigate cyber-risk. For instance, bank supervision includes vulnerability assessments to assess the quality of cyber-risk management, onsite examinations of the financial institution's information and communication technology systems, and the incorporation of information technology auditors in onsite inspections (CBK 2017, 2018).

---

[8]FinTech activities may be considered as part of the "shadow banking" sector, that is, financial intermediaries that provide services similar to traditional commercial banks, but outside banking regulations. As the 2007–08 financial crisis demonstrated, the lack of appropriate regulation in the shadow banking sector, and their vulnerable business model, led to rapid contagion to the rest of the financial system.

The nature of the trade-off between safety-efficiency in regulation of FinTech is evolving (see Box 9). The efficiency-safety trade-off is conceptually very similar to comparable trade-offs that have already been considered by policymakers in the banking industry (Keeley 1990) or the payments industry (Berger, Hancock, and Marquardt 1996). One of the differences with Fin-Tech is the nascent nature of these technologies, which makes it more difficult for regulators and policymakers to determine with reasonable certainty and accuracy the benefits in terms of economic efficiency, and the additional vulnerabilities, side effects, and risks that these technologies can bring to society. Moreover, "inflated expectations" about FinTech that are part of what has been called the "hype cycle" (Gartner 2017) increase the difficulties for regulators to provide a fair assessment of these trade-offs. Continued research is needed to remain up to date with the potential benefits and costs involved in these technologies.

Due to its pioneering efforts in mainstreaming mobile money, sub-Saharan Africa became an early leader in regulatory innovation. Sub-Saharan African countries with large FinTech operations can use their central bank to license and regulate mobile network operators. For instance, in the Kenyan National Payment System Regulations, "mobile payment service providers" are telecommunications service providers licensed under the Kenya Information and Communications Act and authorized by the CBK to offer payment services. The common feature of these regulatory frameworks is that a mobile money network operator maintains liquid assets equal to the amount of money issued electronically. The funds are usually pooled and held by a bank in the name of the mobile network operator. This arrangement ensures a customer's money will be available on demand. Mobile network operators do not typically need to meet minimum capital requirements. Due to the relatively small value of individual transactions, mobile network operators can limit money laundering and terrorist financing risks by capping the number of accounts an individual can hold and by limiting the total value of transactions over a given period, although additional measures are also needed.

The rapid growth and evolution of FinTech created gaps for regulators to address. The rise of FinTech has the potential to create vulnerabilities in the financial system through several channels. First, FinTech should increase competition in the financial system, which could reduce existing financial institutions' solvency by reducing their earnings, and promote higher risk taking (Keeley 1990). Second, if FinTech firms provide financial services, thereby acting de facto as new banks, supervisors may decide to set asymmetric regulations on capital or liquidity, which could generate incentives for regulatory arbitrage and risk shifting. Third, many of these new players may enter in the market with relevant experience from other industries (for example, retail or telecoms), but much lower experience and expertise in the

27

financial industry. This can have negative consequences for the financial system too. All these channels can be an important source of risk, such as credit risk, operational risk, liquidity risk, money laundering/financing of terrorism risk, and other types of risks.

FinTech also raises concerns regarding the emergence of new risks related to money laundering and financing of terrorism. Country authorities typically use licensing/market entry controls and preventive measures—including customer due diligence—transaction monitoring, record keeping, and obligations to report suspicious transactions to assist in deterring and detecting money laundering and terrorism financing. Recent technologies such as virtual assets and related financial services have the potential to spur financial innovation and present some AML/CFT solutions, but they also create new opportunities for criminals and terrorists to launder their proceeds or finance their illicit activities (see the Financial Action Task Force (2015 and 2018). Some innovation may favor anonymity of users and promote a lack of transparency in the financial system. In addition, cross-border payments may become faster, cheaper, and more efficient, which can also help promote financial flows between international crime networks. All these factors are a cause of concern regarding money laundering and financing of terrorism, cyber-risks, and other associated risks.

Financial regulation plays a role in the emergence of FinTech. When considering new FinTech entrepreneurs that provide financial intermediation services, bank supervisors will need to consider how these new players are going to be placed vis-à-vis the financial regulatory toolkit. A first consideration that regulators may need to consider is whether FinTech companies should be regulated like traditional banks or whether it would be optimal to set differential regulations based on proportional application of specific requirements for FinTech companies. For example, there are several regulations that increase the cost of operation of banks but are intended to control risks and increase the safety and soundness of banks. These include requiring capital and liquidity buffers, which would create an opportunity cost for new entrants and impact their profitability. There are several tools that are intended to increase the safety and soundness of the financial system when banks are in a situation of stress, such as the use of lender of last resort facilities or the existence of implicit guarantees and deposit insurance schemes. Issues related to the supervision and monitoring of cyber-security and other related operational risks or AML/CTF issues are especially relevant. Regulators could also facilitate interagency cooperation to clarify the conduct of existing supervision.

To understand risk without hindering innovation, some jurisdictions are adopting flexible regulatory approaches, such as "regulatory sandboxes." A regulatory sandbox is a closed testing environment designed for developing regulatory frameworks for emerging business models such as FinTech. Annex 2 provides a description of one of the first regulations specifically designed for FinTech providers, set in March 2017 by the Ministry of Finance in Mexico, and the case of a new regulatory sandbox created in Mauritius in October 2016.

Box 4. Summary of Technologies and Uses

Technological Foundations	Potential Improvements	Sectors Impacted
Mobile access and the internet		Financial inclusion and deepening
Big data and artificial intelligence	Lower information costs Increase in transparency Incentives to formalize	Cross-border payments
Distributed ledger technologies	Contract enforcement Greater trust	Fiscal and monetary sectors
Cryptography		Promoting transparency and reducing corruption

Box 5. Project Khokha: A Distributed Ledger Technology–based Whole Payment Systems

Project Khokha—initiated by the South African Reserve Bank (SARB)—is a proof of concept that simulated a "real-world" trial of a distributed ledger technology (DLT)-based wholesale payment system using a tokenized South African rand. Project Khokha built on previous global initiatives on DLT-based payments systems such as the Bank of Canada's Project Jasper and other initiatives in Brazil, Europe, Japan, and Singapore (see Annex 1). The SARB (2018) notes that the project provided the opportunity to broaden the DLT skills base in the South African banking industry and laid the foundations for future collaborative work—essential in the blockchain context. The results of Project Khokha show that:

- The typical daily volume of the South African payments system could be processed in less than two hours with full confidentiality of transactions and settlement finality.
- Transactions were processed within two seconds, across a network of geographically distributed nodes, with distributed consensus providing the requisite resilience.
- The SARB was able to view the detail of all the transactions to allow for regulatory oversight.
- There are many issues to consider before the decision to take a DLT-based system into production can be made, including those related to the practicalities of implementation, legal and regulatory factors, and the broader economic impact.

DLT can also enhance security and transparency in the payment system while lowering trading costs. DLT significantly enhances the traceability and reliability of information stored in the ledger. As blockchains are difficult to hack, DLT could be robust against cyberattacks. DLT can also help mobilize a large volume of data and information to better assess credit risk, thus contributing to financial stability. Several central banks are analyzing the use of these technologies to replace existing real-time gross settlement systems. In 2016, Payments Canada, along with the bank of Canada, R3, and commercial banks, started an experiment project, codenamed Project Jasper, to explore a DLT-based wholesale payment system.

Box 6. Monetary Policy Implementation and Mobile Money

The remarkable penetration of mobile money services in the sub-Saharan Africa region and the potential of this technology to evolve into a widely used transaction medium is raising concerns about its effects on monetary policy implementation. Several central banks in sub-Saharan Africa adhere to conventional reserve money programs to target inflation through monetary targets. In these countries, targeting reserve money anchors inflation if the growth rates of the money multiplier and the velocity of circulation are constant (or at least predictable).

It is not clear yet how mobile money can affect the money multiplier and the velocity of money. In principle, any mobile money balances are fully backed by money deposited by the mobile money service provider in a bank, so no new money is created. Banks can use these additional funds to increase their lending, which does create new money, but this is no different from the way in which banks use deposits (Adam and Walker 2015). Mobile money services can also help the unbanked population to have access to other financial services, leading to a greater level of financial inclusion, with positive effects on the money multiplier.

Weil, Mbiti, and Mwega (2012) assessed the impact of M-Pesa on the behavior of monetary aggregates in East Africa, concluding that the monetary policy implications of mobile money have, so far, been negligible in Kenya, Tanzania, and Uganda. Weil, Mbiti, and Mwega (2012) show that the velocity of M-Pesa rises over time, which indicates that users are more inclined to use the system as a transaction vehicle. Nonetheless, Weil, Mbiti, and Mwega (2012) suggest that developments and innovations in this space could fuel the growth of mobile money such that it reaches levels where it could have implications for monetary policy. This study was extended by Ndirangu and Nyamongo (2015), who concluded that mobile money has not affected the conduct of monetary policy in Kenya as the (fast) pace of financial development in the country has not caused structural shifts in the long-term money demand relation. Also, Macha (2013) found an association between the instability of money demand in Tanzania after the introduction of mobile money, with implications for the velocity of money. Aron, Muellbauer, and Sebudde (2015) found only tentative evidence that mobile money in Uganda may exert some downward pressure on inflation.

Using a dynamic stochastic general equilibrium model, Adam and Walker (2015) analyzed whether mobile money has changed the monetary policy environment for the major economies of East Africa. Although mobile money poses challenges to the conventional money targeting approaches used by several central banks across the region, these authors found that the impact of mobile money is likely to be positive and enhance the efficacy of monetary policy implementation. Focusing on the growth of mobile money transactions and balances and its implications for inflation forecasting models in Uganda, Aron, Muellbauer, and Sebudde (2015) found no significant effect.

Box 7. e-Money Floats and Financial Stability

Mobile cellular subscriptions in sub-Saharan Africa continue to grow faster than any other region in the world. At the start of 2017, there were more than 420 million unique mobile subscribers in sub-Saharan Africa, equivalent to a penetration rate of 43 percent (GSMA Intelligence 2017). The high usage of mobile money and its rapid growth requires an effective oversight framework to safeguard public confidence and financial stability.

Five key risks and oversight issues arising from mobile payments have been identified (Khiaonarong 2014). They include the legal regime, financial integrity, fund safeguarding, operational resiliency, and risk controls in the payment system. A key element of the oversight framework in mobile money is management of the float that refers to the balance of e-money, physical cash, or money in a bank account that a mobile agent can immediately access to meet customer demands to purchase or sell electronic money. Management of the float has implications for financial stability. Based on country experiences, the key safeguarding measures could include the following:

1. **Usage restrictions:** Restricting customer funds for money transfers and prohibiting use for other purposes such as extending credit or covering operating expenses of the nonbank entity. Introducing liquidity requirements for nonbank mobile payment schemes, which should include limiting the liquid asset categories to be held that are equivalent to the total value of customer funds collected.

2. **Protection requirements:** Insulating customer funds against the claims of other creditors of the nonbank in the event of its insolvency. Introducing insurance or comparable guarantees of electronic values for nonbank mobile payment schemes. Adopting mechanisms to guarantee traceability of customer funds in the event of mass conversion of electronic values to cash, or potential nonbank failure.

3. **Float management:** A segregated trust account held by a third party with a licensed and prudentially regulated bank. Maintaining multiple accounts at different banks to diversify risks. Holding of other forms of safe assets such as government securities.

Most financial technology (FinTech) companies use their own balance sheet for the provision of credit or other services, implying a relatively minor impact of FinTech on financial contagion through the credit or liquidity channel. However, many FinTech companies have begun to rely increasingly on funding from banks or other financial institutions with implications for interconnectedness risks and financial stability.

Customer funds held by nonbanks may be at risk if unprotected. Financial authorities should consider adopting fund safeguarding measures. In sub-Saharan Africa, mobile operators cannot re-invest floats; in some other jurisdictions (Hong Kong SAR, China),

Box 7. e-Money Floats and Financial Stability *(continued)*

floats are managed by segregation from the stored-value facilities issuer's own funds. By not allowing further investment of floats, regulatory authorities in sub-Saharan Africa have chosen to endure the safety and integrity of mobile payment systems, enhancing financial sector stability.

Box 8. Regulatory and Supervisory Technologies in Sub-Saharan Africa

African countries have developed or are exploring solutions in the areas of regulatory technology and supervisory technology.

The National Bank of Rwanda uses an electronic data warehouse to automate and streamline the reporting processes for the supervision of more than 600 financial institutions, including banks, microfinance institutions, and savings and credit cooperative organizations. Data can be automatically pulled every 24 hours or even every 15 minutes in the case of mobile money and money transfer operators (Broeders and Prenio 2018, Box 1).

The Central Bank of Nigeria and the Nigeria Inter-Bank Settlement System are developing a "data stack" that would include a data warehouse and dashboards and allow risk-based and timely financial supervision and inform new strategies such as financial inclusion policies and regulatory interventions (di Castri, Grasser, and Kulenkampff 2018).

Box 9. The Safety-Efficiency Frontier

A well-known trade-off between safety and efficiency has often been considered for the financial sector. This trade-off, which has been applied to the banking industry (Keeley 1990) or the payments industry (Berger, Hancock, and Marquardt 1996; Chapman et al. 2015), can be simply illustrated by a safety-efficiency frontier possibilities curve. The safety-efficiency frontier and the set of points inside the frontier summarizes the possible set of market structures that may attain various levels of safety and efficiency levels, subject to current regulatory and technological constraints. More specifically, along the frontier, technical efficiency is achieved because a certain market structure cannot achieve more safety without compromising efficiency, and vice versa. Points inside this frontier represent technical inefficiency because there exists an alternative market/technological configuration that could achieve more safety, efficiency, or both. Points above and to the right of the frontier represent market and technological structures that are unattainable given current constraints. Over time, regulatory changes and technological progress create movements of the frontier, making some of these points technically feasible.

This simple framework can be used to analyze the impact of financial technology (FinTech) in broader terms by considering the social impact of these technological innovations. We would expect that FinTech expands the possibilities frontier in terms of efficiency and safety as FinTech providers expand in the value chain. Recent technologies can increase allocative efficiencies by reducing the cost of providing financial services, increasing competition, and adding new services. Also, these innovative technologies can be useful to better monitor risks, reduce operational failures, or provide a solution to emerging vulnerabilities such as cyberattacks and anti-money laundering and counter-terrorist financing. For instance, the blockchain technology is essentially a distributed network database that reduces transaction errors, increases transparency and accountability, and is more flexible than traditional technologies used in clearing, payment, and settlement systems (see International Finance Corporation 2017).

Because FinTech expands the universe of existing opportunities and possibilities in the financial industry, the set of alternatives made available by FinTech are greater than before. One of the main challenges for public authorities is to avoid suboptimal market situations that FinTech could create in the economy. For instance, in Figure 9 we show a market structure in point 1 with a certain balance between safety and efficiency. As technological progress moves the frontier, point 2 would be better off in terms of safety and efficiency. Point 2 represents a market allocation that uses state-of-the-art FinTech to arrive to a point where the cost of providing financial services is smaller, there is more competition, and the financial system has a lower level of vulnerabilities. Suboptimal public policies and regulations could move the allocation to suboptimal point 3, which is a situation that improves point 1 in terms of efficiency, but not in safety.

Box 9. The Safety-Efficiency Frontier *(continued)*

Figure 9. An Efficiency-Safety Trade-Off

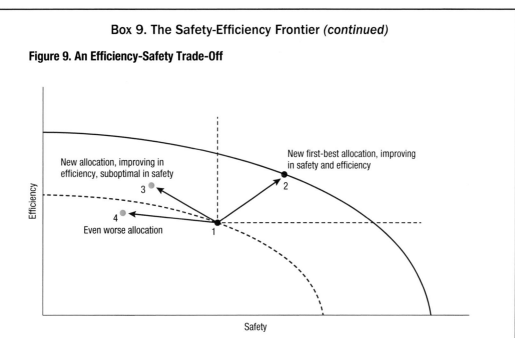

Source: Authors' calculations.

The entry of nonbanks in the financial services industry provides a good example. There could be "excessive" market entry by nonbanks (for example, mobile operators) that significantly increases competition and efficiency in the market but also adds fragility to the financial system. These new players can use their mobile platforms to provide traditional and new bank-related financial services at a lower cost than traditional brick-and-mortar providers. However, their use of innovative technologies (for example, blockchain, mobile money platforms, crowdfunding) can create new vulnerabilities such as cyber-risks or other operational risks. Also, these players may not have adequate regulatory capital levels or have access to central bank lending, which makes them potentially more vulnerable to external shocks. For instance, in sub-Saharan Africa some mobile money providers have started to provide financial services beyond payments, such as savings accounts and microcredits. These providers may not have access to deposit insurance, have limited or no capital, and no access to emergency lending by the central bank. During a crisis of confidence in the financial system, these operators could be exposed to potential deposit runs or to a shortage of other forms of funding, which could lead to failures and contagion to the entire financial system.

4 Conclusions

There is much uncertainty around the ultimate impact of financial technology (FinTech) and policymakers in sub-Saharan Africa as in other regions of the world. At times, the speed of adoption of technology will even be faster in the region, as in the case of the rapid growth of mobile payments. Efficiency considerations include choices regarding competition and coordination (as in the case of whether to push for interoperability), the likely impact on business models and profitability, and cost and inclusion issues. They will also have to manage risks to stability and security (including cyber-risk), and to financial integrity, and consider the possible impact on monetary policy implementation and transmission as well as financial stability issues. Cyber-security is of concern as it is an emerging global risk (International Telecommunication Union 2017).

Policymakers in sub-Saharan Africa will need to address several trade-offs to reap the potential benefits of FinTech. By 2035, more than half of those entering the global labor market will be in sub-Saharan Africa. Technological innovation and infrastructure development can play key roles in allowing the continent to transform its demographic dividend into jobs, growth, and rising living standards for all.

First, policymakers will need to fill the large existing hard infrastructure gap in the region, choose the appropriate mix of energy sources to generate electricity, and improve the governance of public utilities to ensure an adequate provision of electricity and internet services. However, to do so they will need to complement their scarce public resources with domestic and foreign private financing as well as concessional resources. In turn, policymakers will need to mitigate the risks associated with investing in infrastructure projects in their countries (Gutman, Sy, and Chattopadhyay 2015).

Estimates of the infrastructure gap in sub-Saharan Africa need to be updated. Indeed, the oft-quoted figure of $93 billion necessary to fill the region's gap dates to 2009 (Foster and Briceno-Garmendia 2010). Even at $93 billion, there are limits to the use of public financing to address the infrastructure gap, given the level of government indebtedness and low domestic revenue mobilization in the region. Policymakers in the region will need to mobilize the financing needed to invest in electricity generation, transmission, and distribution, as well as in the critical internet infrastructure and the hardware and software systems infrastructure necessary to provide internet services such as fiberoptic links.

Second, policymakers in the region will also need to address the perennial race between fast-moving innovation and the slow pace of regulation. There is a trade-off between catalyzing or at least supporting rapid innovation, which has large potential gains to the economy, and taking the time to identify and manage its associated risks through regulation and supervision to ensure financial stability and integrity. The FinTech sector is evolving rapidly in sub-Saharan Africa, and it is challenging for regulators to identify, measure, and manage the associated risks. However, regulators should be flexible enough not to stifle innovation but at the same time ensure that their objective to maintain macroeconomic and financial stability and financial integrity is not compromised. Since sub-Saharan Africa is dominated by small value payments, proportionality—the balancing of risks and benefits against costs of regulation and supervision—is important and regulators can focus on specific challenges such as price and financial stability, consumer protection from fraud, cyber-risk, and on increasing financial literacy. In anti-money laundering and counter-terrorist financing, efforts to ensure appropriate identification are needed. Regulatory sandboxes are used by many countries and could be a useful approach to follow, while noting that they must be tailored to different objectives, legal structures, and levels of financial development.

Third, policymakers will need to think beyond the potential benefits of FinTech on the financial sector to assess FinTech's impact on employment and productivity, the digital economy, and, more broadly, much-needed structural transformation of their economies. To reap innovation's potential benefits, policymakers will need to elaborate policies that can help leverage human capital such as improving financial and digital inclusion and ensuring the adequate provision of financing to new sectors. Policymakers will need to consider the larger picture as FinTech is only a means to the end of sustainable and inclusive growth. For instance, appropriate education policies should include financial literacy and skills upgrading if a sustainable digital economy with activities such as e-commerce is to be encouraged. Policymakers will need a forward-looking approach to identify the type of future jobs that will be needed in a digital economy and provide the relevant skills and education.

Similarly, they will need to assess how competition in different sectors will affect the landscape of a future e-economy (see Tirole 2017). More broadly, such policy questions should be in the context of the strategy that countries in sub-Saharan Africa are elaborating to transform the structure of their economies to benefit from innovation.

Annex 1. Project Jasper: A Distributed Ledger Technology–based Whole Payment System

Project Jasper built a proof-of-concept system that leveraged a settlement asset issued and controlled by a central bank. The project started by allowing participants to build a settlement capability on a special platform (Ethereum) to demonstrate the ability to exchange a settlement asset between participants. Jasper incorporates a liquidity-saving mechanism that allows participants to coordinate their payments to reduce liquidity needs. Key features of Jasper include the following (see Chapman et al. 2017):

- Value transfer. A financial market infrastructure was made available through a digital representation of currency known as digital depository receipt (DDR) to represent Bank of Canada deposits. DDRs are issued in the system by the Bank of Canada and are backed one for one by cash pledged to the bank by participants. As DDRs are exchanged for central bank money, there is no increase in money circulating in the banking system. DDRs are then used by participants in the system to exchange and settle interbank payments. Ultimate settlement finality on the books of the Bank of Canada is achieved after exchanging DDRs with the Bank of Canada for Canadian dollars transferred into their respective settlement accounts. For all intents and purposes, these DDRs functioned as cash in the system.

- Efficiency. Interbank payments were settled using systems that conduct end-of-day netting between participants. However, as volumes and values increased in these systems, central banks became concerned about the risks inherent in netting. Central banks have responded by implementing real-time gross settlement (RTGS) systems, where payments are processed individually, immediately, and with finality throughout the day. Phase 1 of Project Jasper was implemented as a pure RTGS system, with every individual payment on the ledger being prefunded by DDRs in the participant's wallet. RTGS systems eliminate settlement risk at the cost of an increased need for liquidity. To make RTGS systems less liquidity-demanding, operators around the world have implemented liquidity-saving mechanisms. The most effective liquidity-saving mechanisms are those that support settlement by periodically matching offsetting payments that have been submitted to a central payments queue and settling only the net obligations. However, offsetting algorithms cause delay in settlement, which is unacceptable for some types of payment. Phase 2 of Project Jasper explored the possibility of giving banks the choice of entering payments for immediate settlement or into a queue for netting and deferred settlement.

Annex 2. Financial Technology and Legal Frameworks: The Cases of Mexico and Mauritius

A regulatory framework could provide the legal certainty to support the organization, operation, functioning, and authorization of firms offering alternative means of access to finance and investment, issuance, and management of electronic payment funds, and the exchange of virtual assets. Regulating financial technology (FinTech) could seek to (1) encourage the development of products and services that are covering segments of the market not provided by traditional financial institutions; (2) provide prudential rules in risk—including corporate governance, accounting, and risk management; and (3) prevent money laundering and the financing of terrorism while protecting users of financial technologies. The cases of Mexico and Mauritius can be useful to contrast emerging legal frameworks across countries and regions.

The Case of Mexico

In Mexico, on March 10, 2018, the law regulating FinTech institutions ("FinTech Law") became effective. Key aspects of the law included the following:

- Anti-money laundering and counter-terrorist financing. The law proposes establishing both client and investor identification standards, critical for the integrity and correct functioning of the financial system. To protect investors and clients, FinTech companies will not be allowed to make any guaranteed returns on investment or guarantee the result or success of investments. Also, the initiative prohibits related persons, or those with the power to direct or control a FinTech institution's management or resolutions, from applying for crowdfunding financing, as well as those officers, partners, board directors, managers, and other individuals imprisoned for over one year for a financial crime.

45

- Institutions. FinTech institutions considered under the law include (1) crowdfunding institutions, (2) electronic payment institutions, and (3) virtual asset management institutions. To provide services in Mexico, these FinTech institutions should be legally certified and incorporated as Mexican corporations or limited liability companies.
- Sandboxes. The Mexican law enables innovative companies to operate using technological tools, models, services, or other means through innovative methods or processes. A two-year temporary authorization will be provided (trial period).
- FinTech Council. The law also provides for the creation of a FinTech Council, which shall act as a means of consultation, advice, and coordination with the purpose of creating a space for exchanging opinions, ideas, and knowledge between the public and private sector, to learn about the innovations in the field of FinTech and plan their development and regulation.

The Case of Mauritius

Mauritius is using the concept of "regulatory sandbox" to spur innovation in the FinTech industry by accommodating the entry of new entrepreneurs. The country has avoided adopting a prescriptive approach to regulation and has instead developed a regulatory framework that facilitates "testing grounds" for new digital business models that are not protected by current regulation. The purpose of the sandbox is to adapt compliance with strict financial regulations to the growth and pace of innovation, in a way that does not burden the FinTech sector with rules while also ensuring consumer protection (BBVA Bank 2017). The Mauritius government launched the Regulatory Sandbox License (RSL) on October 20, 2016.

Although the RSL covers any innovative industry, most of the recent RSL successful applicants are in the FinTech industry. For instance, SelfKey has obtained an RSL to develop a digital identity wallet service based on Block-Chain. Other licenses have been issued to an online crowdfunding platform, a medical company producing stem cells, and a financial provider of new investment products for the film industry.

References

Adam, Christopher S., and Sebastien E. J. Walker. 2015. "Mobile Money and Monetary Policy in East African Countries." University of Oxford. Unpublished, April.

Andresen, Svein. 2017. "Regulatory and Supervisory Issues from FinTech." Cambridge Centre for Alternative Finance Conference, June.

Aron, Janine, John Muellbauer, and Rachel Sebudde. 2015. "Inflation Forecasting Models for Uganda: Is Mobile Money Relevant?" CSAE Working Paper 2015–17, Centre for the Study of African Economies, Oxford, United Kingdom.

Bazot, Guillaume. 2018. "Financial Consumption and the Cost of Finance: Measuring Financial Efficiency in Europe (1950–2007)." *Journal of the European Economic Association* 16 (1): 123–60.

Basel Committee on Banking Supervision. 2017. "Consultative Document. Sound Practices: Implications of Fintech Developments for Banks and Bank Supervisors." Bank for International Settlements, Basel, Switzerland, August.

BBVA Bank. 2017. "What is a Regulatory Sandbox?" November 20. https://www.bbva.com/en/what-is-regulatory-sandbox/.

Beck, Thorsten, and Robert Cull. 2014. "Banking in Africa." In *The Oxford Handbook of Banking, Second Edition*. Oxford, United Kingdom: Oxford University Press.

Benos, Evangelos, Rodney Garratt, and Pedro Gurrola-Perez. 2017. "The Economics of Distributed Ledger Technology for Securities Settlement." Staff Working Paper 670, Bank of England, London, August.

Berger, Allen N., Diana Hancock, and Jeffrey C. Marquardt. 1996. "A Framework for Analyzing Efficiency, Risks, Costs, and Innovations in the Payments System." *Journal of Money, Credit and Banking* 28 (4): 696–732.

Broeders, Dirk, and Jermy Prenio. 2018. "Innovative Technology in Financial Supervision (SupTech)—The Experience of Early Users." Financial Stability Institute, FSI Insights on Policy Implementation 9, Bank for International Settlements, Basel.

Cambridge Centre for Alternative Finance. 2017. *The Africa and Middle East Alternative Finance Benchmarking Report.* Cambridge: Cambridge University.

Central Bank of Kenya. 2017. "Guidance Note on Cybersecurity." August.

———. 2018. "Guidelines on Cybersecurity for Payment Service Providers." August.

Chapman, James, Jonathan Chiu, Sajjad Jafri, and Héctor Pérez Saiz. 2015. "Public Policy Objectives and the Next Generation of CPA Systems: An Analytical Framework." Discussion Paper 2015–6, Bank of Canada, Ottawa, Ontario, Canada.

Chapman, James, Rodney Garratt, Scott Hendry, Andrew McCormack, and Wade McMahon. 2017. "Project Jasper: Are Distributed Wholesale Payment Systems Feasible Yet?" Financial System Review, Bank of Canada, Ottawa, Ontario, Canada, June.

Committee on Payments and Market Infrastructures. 2014. "Non-banks in Retail Payments." Bank of International Settlements, Basel, Switzerland, September.

———. 2016. "Fast Payments—Enhancing the Speed and Availability of Retail Payments." Bank of International Settlements, Basel, Switzerland, November.

———, Markets Committee. 2018. "Central Bank Digital Currencies." Bank of International Settlements, Basel, Switzerland, March.

Di Castri, Simone, Matt Grasser, and Arend Kulenkampff. 2018. "Financial Authorities in the Era of Data Abundance—RegTech for Regulators and SupTech Solutions." BFA, RegTech for Regulators Accelerators (R²A), Somerville, MA, August.

Dupas, Pascaline, Dean Karlan, Jonathan Robinson, and Diego Ubfal. 2016. "Banking the Unbanked? Evidence from Three Countries." NBER Working Paper 22463, National Bureau of Economic Research, Cambridge, MA.

Evans, David S., and Richard Schmalensee. 2016. *Matchmakers: The New Economics of Multisided Platforms.* Cambridge: Harvard Business Review Press.

Financial Action Task Force. 2015. "Virtual Currencies: Guidance for a Risk-Based Approach." Paris, France, June

———. 2018. "Regulation of Virtual Assets." Paris, France, October 19

Financial Stability Board. 2017. "Financial Stability Implications from FinTech: Supervisory and Regulatory Issues that Merit Authorities' Attention." June.

Foster, Vivien, and Cecilia Briceno-Garmendia, eds. 2010. *Africa's Infrastructure: A Time for Transformation.* Washington, DC: World Bank.

Gartner. 2017. "Gartner Hype Cycle." www.gartner.com/technology/research/ methodologies/hype-cycle.jsp.

GSMA Intelligence. 2017. "Global Mobile Trends 2017." September.

Gupta, Sanjeev, Michael Keen, Alpa Shah, and Geneviève Verdier, eds. 2017. *Digital Revolutions in Public Finance.* Washington, DC: International Monetary Fund.

Gutman, Jeffrey, Amadou Sy, and Soumya Chattopadhyay. 2015. "Financing African Infrastructure: Can the World Deliver?" Brookings Global Economy and Development, Washington, DC, March.

He, Dong, Ross Leckow, Vikram Haksar, Tommaso Mancini-Griffoli, Nigel Jenkinson, Mikari Kashima, Tanai Khiaonarong, Céline Rochon, and Hervé Tourpe. 2017. "Fintech and Financial Services: Initial Considerations." Staff Discussion Note 17/05, International Monetary Fund, Washington, DC.

Heller, Daniel. 2017a. "Do Digital Currencies Pose a Threat to Sovereign Currencies and Central Banks?" Policy Brief 17-PB13, Peterson Institute for International Economics, Washington, DC.

———. 2017b. "The Implications of Digital Currencies for Monetary Policy." European Parliament, Brussels, Belgium.

International Finance Corporation. 2011. "Stories from the Field—WIZZIT Micro-Lending Pilot (South Africa)." Washington, DC.

———. 2017. "Blockchain: Opportunities for Private Enterprises in Emerging Markets." Washington, DC.

International Monetary Fund and World Bank Group. 2018. "The Bali Fintech Agenda." IMF Policy Paper, Washington, DC, October.

49

International Telecommunication Union. 2017. *Global Cybersecurity Index 2017*. Geneva, Switzerland.

Internet Society. 2017. "Global Internet Report: Paths to our Digital Future." Reston, VA, and Geneva, Switzerland.

Kasekende, Louis A. 2010. "Developing a Sound Banking System in Sub-Saharan African Countries." *African Finance in the 21st Century* 63–86.

Keeley, Michael C. 1990. "Deposit Insurance, Risk, and Market Power in Banking." *The American Economic Review* 80 (5): 1183–200.

Khiaonarong, Tanai. 2014. "Oversight Issues in Mobile Payments." IMF Working Paper 14–123, International Monetary Fund, Washington, DC.

Levine, Ross. 2005. "Finance and Growth: Theory and Evidence." in *Handbook of Economic Growth*, ed. Philippe Aghion and Steven N. Durlauf, 865–934. Amsterdam: Elsevier.

Lukonga, Inutu. 2018. "Fintech, Inclusive Growth, and Cyber Risks: Focus on MENAP and CCA Regions." IMF Working Paper 18/201, International Monetary Fund, Washington, DC.

Macha, Deogratius. 2013. "Mobile Financial Services in Tanzania: State of the Art and Potentials for Financial Inclusion." Unpublished, University of Dar es Salaam, doctoral thesis.

Mancini-Griffoli, Tommaso, Maria Soledad Martinez Peria, Itai Agur, Anil Ari, John Kiff, Adina Popescu, and Celine Rochon, 2018. "Casting Light on Central Bank Digital Currencies." Staff Discussion Note 18/08, International Monetary Fund, Washington, DC.

Mas, Ignacio, and Amolo Ng'weno. 2010. "Three Keys to M-PESA's Success: Branding, Channel Management and Pricing." *Journal of Payments Strategy & Systems* 4 (4): 352–70.

Mas, Ignacio, and Dan Radcliffe. 2011. "Mobile Payments Go Viral: M-PESA in Kenya." Working Paper 54338, The World Bank, Washington, DC.

Matheson, Thornton, and Patrick Petit. 2017. "Taxing Telecommunications in Developing Countries." IMF Working Paper 17/247, International Monetary Fund, Washington, DC.

Ndirangu, Lydia, and Esman Morekwa Nyamongo. 2015. "Financial Innovations and Their Implications for Monetary Policy in Kenya." *Journal of African Economies* 24 (Supplement 1): i46–i71.

Philippon, Thomas. 2016. "The Fintech Opportunity." Unpublished, Stern School of Business, New York University.

Pisa, Michael, and Matt Juden. 2017. "Blockchain and Economic Development: Hype vs. Reality." Center for Global Development, Washington, DC, July 20.

Ratha, Dilip, Supriyo De, Sonia Plaza, Ganesh Seshan, Nadege Desiree yameogo, and Eung Ju Kim. 2018. "Migration and Remittances: Recent Developments and Outlook." *Migration and Development Brief 30*, World Bank, Washington, DC, December

Shapiro, Carl, and Hal R. Varian. 1998. *Information Rules: A Strategic Guide to the Network Economy.* Cambridge, MA: Harvard Business Press.

Skan, Julian, James Dickerson, and Luca Gagliardi. 2016. *Fintech and the Evolving Landscape: Landing Points for the Industry.* Dublin, Ireland: Accenture.

Suri, Tavneet, and William Jack. 2016. "The Long-Run Poverty and Gender Impacts of Mobile Money." *Science* 354 (6317): 1288–92.

South African Reserve Bank (SARB). 2018. "Project Khokha: Exploring the Use of Distributed Technology for Interbank Payments Settlement in South Africa." Pretoria, South Africa.

Tirole, Jean. 2017. *Economics for the Common Good.* Princeton, NJ: Princeton University Press.

Weil, David, Isaac Mbiti, and Francis Mwega. 2012. "The Implications of Innovations in the Financial Sector on the Conduct of Monetary Policy in East Africa." International Growth Centre Working Paper 12/0460, International Growth Centre, London, United Kingdom.